Phantom Laundry

2   Phantom Laundry

BACKLASH
PRESS

A pioneering publishing house dedicated to creating intelligent, vivid books.

Established to inform, educate, entertain and provoke.

Poetry Press

By the same author

The Wanted
Broken Land: Poems of Brooklyn

Phantom Laundry

Michael Tyrell

PRESS

A Backlash Book
First published 2017

Backlash Press
+44(0) 1825 830166
www.backlashpress.com
info@backlashpress.com

Book and Cover Design:
The Scrutineer, Rachael Adams.

Fonts: Adobe Garamond, Bree serif.
Printed and bound by IngramSpark,
on 50lb uncoated paper.

ISBN: 978 1 5272042 6 3

Copyright © Michael Tyrell 2017

The moral rights of the author has been asserted.

All rights reserved. No part of this publication may be reproduced, stored in a retrieval system or transmitted in any form or by any means, electronic, mechanical, photocopying, recording or otherwise, without permission of the copyright holder.

Back cover image: 'Siren 2016' by Michael Tyrell

Acknowledgements

Grateful acknowledgement to the editors of the following, where some of these poems and prose pieces first appeared, often under earlier titles:
All of Them Witches: "Perfect Baby"
Fogged Clarity: "Continually, as October," "With you, hushed pal"
Konundrum Engine Literary Review: "Rooms"
Phatitude: "In Brentwood," "Horse pucky," "In Caesar's month," "Sally Superstion sows"; "Terry Teryaki, alone not lonely"
Scythe: "The blue funk man cometh," "Hardly any talkies," "I fire a salvo," "In the widow and orphan control room," "Save the eight-day-old earth"

*

Michael Tyrell is the author of *The Wanted* (The National Poetry Review Press, 2012) and his poems have appeared in many magazines, including *Agni, The Canary, Fogged Clarity, The New York Times, The Paris Review, Ploughshares*, and *The Yale Review*. With Julia Spicher Kasdorf, he edited the anthology *Broken Land: Poems of Brooklyn* (NYU Press, 2007). He teaches at New York University and resides in Brooklyn, where he was born.

*

Notes

A few lines from "Juvenilia" appeared in my earlier collection *The Wanted* (2012).

In "Resume, Exhausted," the line "Lo in slacks, Dolores on the dotted line" is from Vladimir Nabokov's *Lolita*.

"Looking for Mr. Goodbar" and "Rosemary's Baby" are collages assembled from lines from these movies.

In "Family Album," the line "Sadie giggled. Katie sketched. Leslie looked bored" is borrowed from Vincent Bugliosi and Curt Gentry's true-crime account *Helter Skelter*.

In "Sisters," some lines from Brian DePalma's film of the same title show up in the poem.

"Famous Last Words" shapes itself from interviews that Nick Broomfield conducted with Aileen Wuornos in his documentary *Aileen: Life and Death of a Serial Killer*.

Blackberrying

From between two hills a sudden wind funnels at me,
Slapping its phantom laundry in my face…

Sylvia Plath

Phantom Laundry

Contents

I. Perfect Baby	/15
II. Phantom Laundry	/25
Brevity is the Soul of Laundrette	/25
Inner Tube	/26
Americannery	/27
Elegy	/28
Will You Marry It	/29
Resume, Exhausted	/30
Are We Here Yet	/31
Last Wash	/32
Angels of History	/33
Brand-Name Bardo	/34
Where the Morning Pours Gold through Finger-Streaked Glass Doors	/35
Eh, Put the Lame One In	/36
Spirits and Whispers	/37
Pacific Heights	/38
Sisters	/39
Nights and Weekends	/40
Looking for Mr. Goodbar	/41
Genesis	/42
Holiday Special Children	/43
Penelope and Others	/44
Necessity, Invention	/45

Wetness Protection	/46
Tearoom Insider Trading	/47
Famous Last Words	/48
Pinned Bulletin	/49
Rosemary's Baby	/50
Namedropping (1)	/51
Desolate Housewives	/52
For Frances Elena Farmer	/53
Ode to Onan	/54
Flip, Scan, Replay	/55
Juvenilia	/56
Rewriting Persephone	/57
Best Wishes of the Flu Season	/58
Namedropping (2)	/59
Prayers for the Global Warmers	/60
First Frost, New York	/61
For the Losers in Fairy Tales	/62
Valentine	/63
Divorce, Mon Amour	/64
Without Wings	/65
Have You Checked the Children?	/66
Mirror	/67
Mad	/68
Surgical Reflections	/69
Promissory Note	/70

Canine Songs	/71
Wireless	/72
Goth-Rock Youth	/73
Family Album	/74
The Descending	/75
III. Rooms	/76

14 Phantom Laundry

I. Perfect Baby

The baby still exists. Is existence the same thing as survival? One implies the stationary, the other the aggressive. Whatever. The baby exists, it survives, it uses the back yards, gardens, alleys, and abandoned lots of our neighborhood in Brooklyn. Many believe the baby is a ghost, but some claim to have got near it enough to pick it up. The baby has been known to bite. It has a full set of adult, sharp teeth. Photographs of both the baby and the bites have been proved spurious. And it looks like any other baby, perfect in its imperfection, so taking a picture of it wouldn't really tell you a great deal. The eyes are blue, they cry real salt. It moves and it wants to go somewhere, but it doesn't seem to want to belong to anyone or anything.

Maybe it's playing a trick on us. You know those empty carriages you see on the sidewalk? Well, the baby likes to crawl into them and wail until a stranger comes along and trundles the baby to the police station. Of course, by the time the stranger has entered the precinct and has filled out the necessary forms the baby has vanished.

The baby is older than many grown ups. If it is alive and has been alive and seemingly ageless for so long, it must be a freak. But it has not been immobilized, pickled for display. It simply didn't become something else, the way all babies are supposed to change into someone else.

It broke the law and stayed hungry and angry. That cost it a home and a name. What does it live on? When we leave food for the skeletal cats that cower beyond reach, under cars or behind gates, does it eat this? Does it pick through our garbage? Have the animals taken it in, nursed it until it sucked them dry?

Everyone has heard about the baby in Australia who was taken by the dingo. But maybe it was the baby who took the dingo. I've heard that the mother of the dingo baby is now hosting television programs about animals. Maybe she's still trying to find her baby, her Azaria, a name mistakenly translated by the press as "sacrifice in the wilderness." We have to stop relying on the mistaken assumption that babies are defenseless. Maybe some of them have a secret poison behind their eyes, like toads. If they can't fight, maybe some of them can at least will themselves to die.

It's inevitable but reprehensible that for some of us the baby has become a kind of vermin. There have been sightings of it crawling on the sides of buildings, clinging to brick and concrete. Crawling somewhere, always crawling. It doesn't walk. Where does it go in rain and snow? We are an old neighborhood and can't guarantee that every building is kept safe from the baby. We have deployed various poisons, but we don't want to take responsibility for human casualties. We can't promise that derelict buildings don't exist where the baby can seek refuge.

Enter the baby at your own risk. It is like a condemned building. We also come to the issue of communicable diseases. "Every baby is a germ factory," one anonymous source said.

Every once in a while a skeptical journalist or a coolheaded social worker materializes, looking for the baby. The baby must be traceable. Surely someone could not come into the world devoid of a record. Someone must have put it out, the way people will sometimes put a baby in a dumpster. We'd like to believe that it's the records that get thrown out more often than babies.

I wait for the baby at my window, I wait for the baby to interrupt the construction men putting up the condominium next door, I wait for the baby to be caught and dissected by a kind doctor who says she couldn't help it, the baby couldn't be saved.

It might be there is more than one baby.

"The theory that there is always one of these running around is ludicrous," said a man who wrote a book about the baby. He was being interviewed on TV. "These stories have been around for thirty, forty, fifty years."

Mutant babies—perhaps nuclear devices were detonated in Brooklyn, or an expectant mother took a dip in the toxic-waste contaminated Newtown Creek.

I leave a carriage out for the baby, but someone else wheels it away. Damn.

The baby has been known to wear various masks and wait at the end of long hallways. The woman who recently closed her toy shop claimed that she was horrified to discover one of her dolls moving when she picked it up. It was the baby, a great master of disguise.

It could be that the baby is the reincarnation of Houdini, the Buddha, Christ, or the opposite of Christ. Our society's spiritual decomposition has caused it be in a kind of a stasis. It cannot grow up to dazzle us or destroy us, so it stays in one form. To what—

warn us? It's Hamlet as an infant, unable to pick up a sword. It's Lear caught out in the storm, and each of us are the fools. Perhaps. Causes of its inability to grow and take its place as a useful citizen (hence someone who can be used, sacrificed if necessary) could include malnutrition, lead paint poisoning, genetic defects, the obsession with the celebrity culture, the failure of public agencies and officials, poor parenting skills, the language barriers that are not really barriers but mazes.

The baby is actually the last survivor of an aboriginal civilization buried under Brooklyn, a lost city of gold. This was so many millennia ago. The oracle of the civilization foresaw genocide and destruction. The people voted and the gods answered: the civilization was collapsed into this one mysterious being: an act of divine defiance. Something minor, but all the same impossible to remove.

There could be a reality-television show about the baby and our attempts to look for it. We could use a kind of special tracking device that the baby would ingest in the food we'd leave for bait. We could watch its mysterious progress on a radar screen. We could have people compete to see which one would find it first. There would be various methods—gluetraps, nets, Tasers, teargas. Part of the suspense would be debating whether the baby would be captured alive. Viewers would make online or hotline wagers. The prize would be one million dollars, but not the baby itself. The baby would have to be saved for season two. DNA tests could be conducted on the saliva traces on the food. Perhaps the DNA would link the baby to the royal families of Europe or some Hollywood royalty, or perhaps it would prove to be like the red rain of Kerala reported a few years back, proof of the theory that life came from an extraterrestrial source.

One thing's for sure. Everyone wants a piece of the baby, but it's a whole baby and cannot be cut in half. Because it really is a perfect baby. It is an organism that will not grow to reproduce, that will consume and consume but it is a baby and that is an innocent consumption, and you can't really put it in the same category of ruthless consumption that the rest of us live by. Someone wanted to pass on their genetic material, but the baby thwarted that. It rewrote history. It has upset the balance. It has ruined so many potential franchises and has made so many women infertile and so many men incapable of achieving an erection.

Maybe this is why the baby is wanted in connection with a series of conspiracies. During the Cold War it was a Communist baby, now it's an Al-Quaida baby. It could even be the urban-legend baby on the plane, the one that's stuffed with smuggled cocaine.

Obviously, a movie about the baby is in the works. Open auditions have been held, but the casting director violated a union law involving the auditioning rules concerning children and the production has been halted by longwinded litigation. It's just the latest setback. The movie has been so long in development that various actors, many of them bald and fat and dead, such as Marlon Brando and Orson Welles, have been associated with the project.

Many seemingly ordinary women have stepped forward to say, "The baby is mine, therefore the guilt and the suffering are mine also." Not all of these women have proved to have female genitalia.

I hate the baby. The baby stinks, it stinks like shit and death. It was probably left out in the elements the way the ancients left the useless babies outside to die.

I love the baby. I am told to love helpless things; if I saw it on the subway platform I would dive down to rescue it. It has a full brain and maybe even more, unlike those babies born only with a brainstem who cry for a month and die. Just a brainstem—a medulla oblongata to control involuntary functions, but nothing to switch on motion or consciousness. Not this baby—it might have more than one brain.

No question: it fills something in our lives, even if we have our own children. We have to let our children go. Who doesn't want something to tell him that he'll live forever? They don't give us what we want. They want us where they once were when they were babies: wheeled in the carriage, helpless, then put away for the night. I put the baby down for the night, it has been so often said. Put down can also mean euthanasia. Just last year many dogs were put down for carrying a rare virus. These are the elements of love, in some cases: knowing when to kill what you love.

The baby is rustling in the leaves somewhere, looking for a place to settle down for the night. Its favorite baby is the Lindbergh baby, whom it is convinced is still alive somewhere.

The baby has baptized itself in church, at night, unofficially. Limbo is a place for babies. Our neighborhood is one such Limbo.

There are times when I must surrender what I want to say, bite my tongue. I could call the police, but they have stopped answering calls related to the baby. Every day real babies are being flung out of windows, abused, kissed and adored, cooed over, photographed when they are still a cluster of cells.

Years pass by without mention of the baby. I'm so disgusted that I paid so much money to subscribe to that The Ghost Baby of Greenpoint electronic newsletter and it doesn't even give updates anymore. For my part, I remain childless, a bachelor, someone who passes by the babies of the world and clears the subway stairs so that women with strollers can have the right of way.

Babies age you. I've noticed that. They strip the face from the skull and fold it many times, a sort of origami, until it is lined and creased sufficiently, and then they hand it back to you. It looks like a tortilla that's been prepared by an incompetent chef. It doesn't fit right. I'm babyless and I've stayed young, by comparison.

But occasionally a hand, maybe the baby's, reaches out in the darkness, tells me my skin is soft. I'm called an infant as a term of affection, seduction. (The touch is real, but hearing the person say "baby" might be an auditory hallucination.) Then I feel that my own name fades away like the letters on those trick cups that lose words when you pour the hot liquid in.

But that's a cop-out, because I haven't told you my name. I haven't even acknowledged your presence till now, but now that the pronoun's out it sticks to everything.

The word you is like come being shot at you in the dark, when it's your first night in the reformatory and this onslaught is your welcome, your initiation.

You are like the child being read to by someone you cannot see, who has crept into your room at night. But you scare me so. Maybe you are out *there* somewhere, reading these words. Somewhere distant, like a military outpost in Antarctica, watching the permafrost melt. Or maybe it is you have crept in to see me, to take what you want. I sit on my bed telling you this story, but you cannot see my mouth move, you cannot see what I look like. The bed feels heavier with you on it, but not so heavy. Maybe I underestimate the power and scope of your perception. You could be making faces at me in the dark because you see how scared and exhausted I look, or worse, you could be someone without a face, a kind of living blank page unless I picture an ideal reader with very specific, attractive features.

We are alone together regardless. You are utterly vulnerable, utterly silent, and yet you may harm me. I have told you about the baby and that is the best I can offer. I am no authority on the baby. Because it is not meant to resemble anyone living or dead. Because it is a baby, something utterly devoid of a personality and therefore easy to love. You may pick it up and infect it with whatever emotion you like—your emotion, not its, not mine. Do you have any questions? Probably not. Clearly, I cannot be with you for an instant without your knowing everything that I'm about. There's money in the knife drawer and you can get a knife too, if that's your wish. Just make it quick. If not, can we still be friends? For as much as I want you to be, you are definitely not the baby I had in mind.

II. Phantom Laundry

Brevity is the Soul of Laundrette

Born from Tide foam a possessive headless case, loofah-starved Aphrodite sandwiched between her agony columns, marble caking her curve balls. Her matinee idle's a son of the bleach who weighs his Moses bundle of tighty whiteys and unbound blacks. His french ticklers riot in revolution, his boxers bruising his jockeys. Love's debriefed. Ball up what draws others to him, deliver the suit of the union before pink-eyed spring drops her American Beauty bloomers, throw the Babylon out with the hard water.

Inner Tube

In the widow and orphan control room, use the Why Sures and Dires at your own risk. The Incredible Hulk on the small scream is all the rage cable basics can afford. We interrupt this programmed cell death to bring you homicide bullets and snakes in the Burger King ballpit. Species guests walk on waves of applause before the live studio absence. Station identity theft on the hour, the test of the emergency caste system, lip-locking collagen untouchables not ready for prime time. Sudsers age rugrats in Lassie years before mailroom on Monday and boardroom on Friday, via bedroom on Wednesday. After forgetting her amnesia, why does Erica Cocaine marries eight Henrys? To change her name and win eight golden trophy heads. Only bloody procedurals and prime reality real estate on Must Seize TV, but how my potty mouth waters for soap at night.

Americannery

If you do not wish here, do not die here. Trade my cherry-chopping, Wooden-Toothed Father Country for the Gopher and Ocean territories, toss in my Outer Where and my unmentionables, my Banana Republicans, my near extinct American Eagles, my Urban Legend Outfitters, usery all my fifty and most unvisited colonies in a line-up of loose slivers in grooves, scald my lukewarm waiters, spin the permanent depressions until the colors run out of analog time and the human wrinkles appear. Wet and cold my country, where the softener seeps in but the powder burns still in washing tone.

Elegy

I love the one leftover bastard sock. The unknown sock who died for the body of his country, even an Achilles shitheel. A petition please, a memorial for the unknown lone tube, fluted column, a hole for the piggy to go broke to stroke market. Celebrate new rationed holiday, every year you get a sock monkey good for stowing ganja and Malibu Stacey valentine notes. The annual sock and buskin of barefoot ballerinas breaking a toe en pointe. In your stocking feet cross the live coals, the ones you got last Christmas in the toe of the Santa booty. Knocking socks off entails some pussyfooting. Good stockings breathe, but don't hold your breath. Or just put a sock in it and grow a pair.

Will You Marry It

Open twenty-four or 420. Where claw machines drop on endangered effigies, little devils learn to hunt Raygun, Speed Freak, Little Red Raiding Hoodlum. Serfs on the Worried Wide Web will find wank for independent hands to do. Ever the dewy mountains and Fujis and white rocks, and sirens louder than Woodstock colors screaming blotty blue murder if you grab these fizzy elixirs. A quarter gets a whole rubber ball or a gold toy that rings true and green on the pretend bride's finger.

Resume, Exhumed

Work at the dummy corporation, make dummies and topiary the hedges, wear casual but know biohazard's better. Silkwoods have been axed to make silk Oxfords, eunuch forms must rinsed and repeated be in weekly absolutions. Lo in slacks, Dolores on the dotted line. An out-of-body auto reply pulls in from the mainframe mystics. Power suitable only for the insoluble dry gleaners who launder dough and drink blood money, waving red sheets to ire the iron bull. Fortune bank-tellers keep baker's hours, sweeping clean the deck and scouring the starved constellations for stark breakers and the Gipper in Heaven who videotapes a spot for GE's new miracle machine.

Are We Here Yet

No gullible travels here. Island package deals abandon ship from held-up, licked-page magazines. Street filmstrips monogamy, day dog wretching on bungee. Stare into the wishwashy glass, a convex crystal ball, no five-star last resort vista but a plenty for woolgathering. Hear me out: airplane window, refracted nosebleed waitresses and the dozing economy classroom, then a downward gawk into the Land of Lakes thick with lords of flies, the surge pissing out the meth labs and crop circles but not the hard-won Bunyan crop.

Last Wash

Folderol, squares for the hips, patchwork family smears from Chef Boyardee or a white picket family's house hubby's tuna helper. Said Lady MacDonald, screw the curdled milkshake container to the utility pole's sticky post. What tenderness in smoothing over the delicacies, overalls and overnothing arguments. Noggin's a sleeve or a sieve in the laundry. That's why a water-logged call-log phone stays in lining, pocket darkness a staycation photo-op. Blue genes predict illness and genius, the Oshgoshbegones. Lost receipt for iceberg, adopted a highway. When runs out of hands, puts mouth where the money went, taken and running.

Angels of History

In Caesar's month, with Caesar's wife a year from grassy-knoll
Dallas and pillbox hat, Marilyn relaxed her pillowcase blondes on
Egyptian cotton. Conspiracy a high thread-count, heads will role
in Cuba and the See Eye Ape. Why was the nurse running the
washer when the fuzz blew in? Bleaching the deathbed linens where
the something gave, where the Camelot brothers briefly flashed
their Excaliburs between the sheaths. When in Rome, put asp to
coliseums like coal-eyed Liz, Eddie Fisher go belly-up. In come
waterbeds then hardly ever, the swinging sixties a stone pendulum
when Monica's jizzed dress becomes Kenneth Starr's witness.
Dribble night-club soda, knead salt from Lot's wife into the blotch
but lay off the sweet gash, our duvets and dirndls and lemonades
make virgin again.

Brand-Name Bardo

Heart, red candy between I and New York on the boy-beater, heart my bare-knuckle boxer, my Alcatraz, the great old god Pan-Am is dead! Fallen the Great Alexander, taken the Belle from the Atlantic, the Atlantic married to the Virgin, in every plane the No Smoking sign eternally burning. The Wiz was beat in the end, his outlet oz's windows soaped over, and my wool's worth can't get be got in a city scattered with Domino's and Subways at ground level. Chemical or Fleet, the Fog Bank still rolls in, enduring painful withdrawal for a rare euphoric deposit deficit. If only the voicestream were real, chill fountain to baptize the toes hoofing makes numb and the fingers that grow me numbers. Aphrodite's Cleaners, mergered and acquisitioned by a red-eye one-night stand messenger, giving birth to Hermaphrodite. All, the red-pepper colored bottle promises, All the ever-loving mother of Nothing, a phrase only a mother could.

Where the Morning Pours Gold through Finger-Streaked Glass Doors

The Till Man puffs his Camel for energy and so. Baby mamas or tweens done puttering. No client beside me, a B-side, I was and am besides myself, the rumpled stilts and skin all shrunken. Even the alone's not quite. At best some chip off the old city's Eeyore eyeless as Oedipal underwear in the Dust and Frowning bin. Fork-tongue poster warns that few in management take some blame for lost or damaged eyesores. The light FM tines of tinfoil on fillings.

Eh, Put the Lame One In

Singles, bars, counter throat culture. Prince Albert, Jack the Ripper, weak fabricator, champ shredder. Love and carriage sittin in a family tree, first comes fire department. Wedding weak wires finding two of everything, bi one get wanton free. Not the best man, only a groomed horse. Hard luck for the girl to be the apple of her man's eye before the Sera Money, one question popped like a mylar bubble. Want my sickness and health, must be a hitcher who cocks the thumb and clips the flipping bird.

Spirits and Whispers

Hardly any talkies in the underworld. In lieu of speaking ill of the dead soak them again in Lethe before wearing once more for old time's stack. The ropes between tenements sheeted with phantom laundry sheets now. Let the glass not look so a spook don't find a likeness to its liking. Sages smudging the threshold and cartouche with themselves, frottage and some enchantment. Oiling their hands as the Tin Man did, a lid put on the voices of hinges who whine for the last word.

Pacific Heights

Advice from Hitchcock to a fan: if baths and showers scare your wife, take her to the cleaners. The teachers of English object to the tag The Birds is Coming. Later Hitch hands Tippi's girl Melanie a Barbie in a wooden box that Melanie reads as Mommy in coffin. Mad birds not enough for Tippi, she and Melanie make a flick called Roar about lions, MGM cats that bellow about Art for Part's Sake. Then Pacific Heights, where Melanie spies on Tippi's character through binoculars, a facelifted debutante who bumps uglies with Keaton, not Buster or Diane but Michael. Characters who make waves sink without trace. Better the fringe side, not rocking boats. Stay off the corpse-it ladder, Belushi, if you want to keep the topless girl in the animal's house.

Sisters (1976, Brian DePalma)

The blue funk man cometh, two-faced January, cross-eyed squatter. Come as far as Gilmore's jailhouse bride I have, eyeballing the washing machine's transom. Pepto-pink mini bikini a salmon in a sere riverbed. Bakery next door makes gingerbread men not for catching, skedaddle instead back to railroad room for a splatter picture with the Lois Lane actress before she was Lois Lane. Favorite scene in the Staten Island madhouse? The patient who declines to take the ringing baby from the cradle. Thinks germs swim right through the wires. That's how I got sick, talking on the telephone. I never call and I never answer.

Nights and Weekends

Mother Load's ready, can't you go punch the red button, get the hell-heat out of the kitchen? Them spin doctors impatiently heave the gross national products from the vortex. Chicken cages on wonderless wheels a free ride for children who color safe, inside the true lies. Sheep down for the count, the closed circus TV never gets any shut-eye. Wool wants to be a compound of light.

Looking for Mr. Goodbar (1977, dir. Richard Brooks)

Terry Teryaki alone not lonely, rather be seduced than comforted. Tried all night. Busy, busy, busy. Mothergrabber. Candlefucker. Hiya suckers. Taken for a hooker by a pimp and played for a sucker by a dick. Like you, light and dark, on and off, now I seed you, now I don't. Honolulu Hilton, hula hula, hallelujah, happy new year before the cockin cockroaches take over the world. Ah yes love, here lies love and lies, lies, lies. Love don't move the balloon, fuck and punch do. Volare. Oh. Oh.

Genesis

Save the eight-day-old earth by putting back the dirt. Ring around the collar leads to pocket full of paunchus pilate. Lux the sinners, treat the sin. With new Blizzard Pen, hell freezes over, grass blood lifting to go back when none misses them. My untickled ivories, once pearl-cream white, are turning Listerine green. I'm failing much bitter now. Illegal to dump an urn, don't down fall. Where the duds go milky and hair bungs every drain.

Holiday Special Children

Sally Superstition sows her acres with salt, Loveless Lucy pelts sniveling Linus with insecurities like a hausfrau beating area rugs against rocks, Patty Pepperspray gets filthy rich making dirty bombs, no longer a germaphobe Schroder scales the piano with his skin flute, Brown Charlie rinses in secret his skid marks, Neutered Snoopy keeps nose clean, and poor Pigpen dies of smut, pollution rising from his carcass, sooty clouds no Peanut can decipher.

Penelope and Others

Once a pig always a pig, the traveling hero from Icky The proves his wife's loyalty by carving the marital bed from the trunk of a living cyprus. A wet nurse's washed his feet, uncover a childhood nick. All the unsuitables lie in a heap like sprayed roaches. Moly's torn and most whole.

Necessity, Invention

In Brentwood, house of Crawfish, if you clean a floor, you have to move the tree. Buys three-hundred dollar dresses her daughter treats like some dishrag. Rare steak kept for breakfast means vitamins, wire hangers twist into reasons well known to them for disinheritance. Comets over the bathroom tiles, Christina sees stars if that flaw is not spotless, spits out box-office poison.

Wetness Protection

Hell other people's metaphors: as a whistle, wipe the slate, one's plate, a hound's tooth, my bill of health, squeaky. The snow a falling pinheaded angel with a dirty slush Cagney face, losing features into the gravy rain. One, two, wet my overshoe, the goody on the sidewalk's not fit for human contamination. Picnic afters, ants checking into the red velvet Waldorf cake. Salt of the earth or dregs, fruit-fly and multiply. Mornings the grounds all drink from.

Tearoom Insider Trading

Horse pucky, the Golden Shower rule that makes all men aim for the pink deodorant puck. A starbuck for their thoughts, a check signed with triple X's for their tearoom trade. Born with a for a good time caul. Circumseam in the Chiquita, steamed meat mates teams. In the sauna the circle of horny glories speedo the plowing for a foreskins game. The one who dies little first, wins.

Famous Last Words

I'm Cammie Lee Marsh Green who tried to Warn Yous, Eye Rack or Eye Rave or Eye Ran will nuke ya, thanks for using my ass as railroad. Glad I'm sailing away with the rock, pricked by Governor Bush's reelection jazz needle. Bought a pressure cleaning business for my first girlfriend, with everything I had she ran off. Lewis Fell for me after I beat him with his Cain and Abel. Should be burned then cleaned, some scumbags are like that. Said he was saving my eyes for the grand finale and I lost ties over this. At BCI, Mrs. Delicate Cauter trashed all grievances and turned the pressure up on the com. Ninety-nine point forty-four mendacious lies from Republican Pictures. One time I didn't wash my food off was sick two weeks almost died. They were using sonic pressure, crushing my head in. Jesus is going to be there, all the Angel Islands. It's gonna be more like an episode of Star Wreck.

Pinned Bulletin

Put another courter in and try again, Hipstina and Hipstopher need to dry their Converse and Reversible takeovers. Bullied by the communally bored. Button the Kitten lost on Thank God it's Good Friday, 1960. Murse and Manny seeks full-time full-of-yourself empowerment. Good with animal magnetism and stepford alien children of the corn. Joanie loves ChaCha despite his pitstains.

Rosemary's Baby (1968, dir. Roman Polanski)

All of them witches, what they must spend on robes and jewels, pierced ears and piercing eyes, his father's eyes. Can no longer associate myself. Easy, easy, you've got me too high. Not mad about the good luck smell, hate the basement for giving creeps but must clean Hutch's crepes and Guy's New Yorker shirts. There's a closet behind that secretary, I know there is. Typhoon! Try chalky undertaste and snips and snails and saperstein's tails, milk or no milk. Bitten by a chocolate mouse don't change the program on my account. Try to sleep. They'll be waiting. Up on deck.

Namedropping (1)

Karma Sutures Lethal Sequels laughing all the way to the Burbank. Instigate wardrobe malfeasance, retrace Bran Pit Stop maleware insensitivity chip. Marlon wants electric eel power for his jalopy streetcar in Paris. Phoenix, cruise away from Viper. Reese right Jack Nicholson and Jill in Hall, Streeping the Goldie Horn Lox. Collapsing stars: Efron Ephron Eff Bomb; Joan of Arkham Asylum. Such Miss Spent pilot season in Model Ford clinic where learned some Copenhagen skills. It's Sunday the Fifteenth and all the slash and burn teens are driving over the missed daisies. House of greenspan, red graves, this Chinese theater disclosed for mainstreaming.

Desolate Housewives

All the alewives and fishwives; the furniture husbands not even solid enough for lumbar support; the bowling-champion trophy wives, who become burnished drudges; the animal husbandry, no matter how paltry or cockeyed the act of cockbreeding for cockfighting, all must be declared; the one whom I can deduct as dependant, grant green card or pear-shaped baguettes from Zale's in SoHo; whom I can keep house with long enough to be ruled by the common law; who prove that Eros and Errors are sister-wives like polygamous Mormons, or like wives-in-law, the pricy Brazilian-waxed street girls who share day-of-the-week bling and the same shiny pimp-daddy.

For Frances Elena Farmer

I fire a salvo in the electronic bidding war for Frances Farmer's Anarchist Cookbook. Too many parents ebbed her tide, raged her rhythms. How could the Golden toast of new york boy come and forget her? Set on boulevard, sun rise for some on highway. With Little Sister acting all Big Brother, there would rarely be a morning. Ghost appearances on This is Your Life and Today before she died, had a show she once called Frances Farmer Prevents. No Escape? AKA I Escaped from Nazis. As the blackbird in the spring, neath the widow tree. I'm like her now. Clean now, never been so clean. God died a useful thing.

Ode to Onan

Spun and spent and one sea fits all. Nines moons in the before you can say knife. Birth's a decent exposure, maybe the only. Twelve groundhogs later it emerges: my hairy palms, my blindnesses, my slippery second tense. I plead the filth. If hands are brothers, one brother's the better keeper, one washes the missing other and both save the face. Don't fill out a report for tadpole massacre, yet paper trails me to the spanking new.

Flip, Scan, Replay

Results may vary when drywashing brain and preshrinking head, but the plate in my head matches well my dish saddled with light. My lint filter's a platter of Cosby sweater thread. O mother city of assassin initials: JFK, JR Ewing. Heidi projects runaways in miniskirt challenges and elimination rounds, Archie Bunker earns a chair in malapropism. Mary Hartman, married heartland. Blighted rosies, riveting, keep us in stitches, thornbirds in our side. Give me your Tupac and Cobain.

Juvenilia

And those were the children who nab the clothes in the morning, gussied up the depilated grownup trees. Mufflers overalls underthings all the heretics and penitents, whole hometown plucked from a line where it can't know it's waiting, all the king's dark horses and straw men. The blue hour that leaves black and blues will Etch-a-Sketch gnarly shadows like a kind of puberty. Mute funds chime payoffs, penalties and solitudes appreciating like piggy bank savings accounts. But nevermind. That's a never better than a letter. Minus girdles and straps, trappers and worms in this early bird's light, these few. And some like flowers attract mouths without a stink-eye window factory to bark On the Double.

Rewriting Persephone

According to child labor lore, adorable germ factories get to be the sweat shops we buy into, seeing as a mother from earth, not hell, guarantees the northern hemisphere's underweather. Her weaned daughter's so hooked on Pom juice fixed with antioxidants, she can't get out from under, no choice but to divide her fickle year like a bicoastal: fifty Bel Air and fifty Empire building, at Valentine night choke-cherry-red as the pinpoint on a dopefiend's hypodermic.

Best Wishes of the Flu Season

Gotta love the laptop commuters on the Allied Double Ark. Two of everyone, 'nough antibody soap to dry up the West Nile. Best wishes of the flu season, overgrown with touch-me-knots landings. Bedroom communities, seemingly immune, not to be sneezed at. The chicken pox crossing Abbey Road, Ringo around the Rosie, pocket full of EmergenCee. Viscous, viscous. We all glob now.

Name-Dropping (2)

About when Hawke Wins Lit, Titanic crashes into a Goldberg,
makes goldmine out of cold drowned pauper and pawed little rich
girl. Lazarus begot Krueger and Myers, Voorhees and Leatherface.
Queen L. croons I'll Be Seeing You but audiences like you can't see
faces the Academy wants remembered. No clips of performance
captures either. Starlet Blockbuster thanks secret agent, God. Her
Anne Frank's a flower in the attic.

Prayers for the Global Warmers

Back to School by the Fourth of July according to the ads, or summer got busted. Time to get wrapped up in some names. The bait and switch of hybrid seizures such as false fall, carnivorous Wintour. At least in the Where's Waldo heaven no planet's unpronounceable, sky crowded out with horny gods's annihilated nymphs. Losers are keepers. Bad hurricane's labels get relegated to some hell of fame.

First Frost, New York

Continually, as October weeds out the majority of false Edens, the hollow Eve finds us sweet teeth bobbing for apples. Scratch us so we can start over, so we can turncoat through iron-maiden turnstiles. Crosstown ride where the Lord give uth and take uth away, flasher whose jimson got jammed in slamming doors. We might miss an apocalyptic eclipse, but the river-frontiers burst in the Eerie Canals. House and Garden Reader's headphones corkscrewed as snakes whisper out, get the hell.

For the Losers in Fairy-Tales

In the woods that yes-man Simon's yesterday's noose for Hangman. House and home eaten out of, can all the burnt-orange Dorito crumbs still hurry us there? So many wolves proved delusional, the granny's postmortem turning up no outre canines or bodies in the body like nesting dolls. Little men no more snap in half, blood never fills shoes, plots and pockets can grow no further holes. Apple in little parings that won't lodge in the virgin's throat to make her a pretty museum mummy. No rampion to hanker after, no firstborn regifted since the woods went paperless, ungreen. See the omega witch in her high-rise kitchen pining for meat condoned under some former regime? Where there is hexing the substitutes, also thankful for the oven none can heave her into. Her barred balcony over a buxom city isn't, to her soundless mind, female. Among the jackpot of punishing lacks she fingers a thread of ivy feigning a once upon a time braid.

Valentine

Yes, My Space is a great antibacterial against viral video invasion, Facebook features are optional, inbox never gets unwrapped, instant massages the ego and sexting sets its own privates policy, but revenge is still a cold best gotten from a kiss.

Divorce, Mon Amour

Syndicated sob sisters say no way to calling shared pets after book titles. He's wifeless now, the guy who once owned two tortoiseshells and with his wife named them Kama Sutra. One in the loft, one with the ex, he's stuck with half a guide, as if some saw had severed Holy from Bible. So many hoarders and bibliomancers who use animals and tomes like familiars to make spells that don't work. Everything his wife didn't take he gave away or hocked, is how he closes. Others put on continuity this pair put together. Recollections crabby as lice that have burrowed in all be scalded away by us usurpers of the used. His and hers now ours.

Without Wings

With you, hushed pal, in hideous library atrium in winter. Your winter not my hypothermia, your changed-topic hush not my silent treatment, your engine not my station. Thank you, powerless chum, maybe I'm sorry? Only a leather couch we sit on, not the blood ox skinned for it, only the army of bookworms murmuring through metal detectors and not a pack for a lover to cut a rival from. Returned volumes thud in their aluminum bin: not a crypt. No references to leapers from the balcony who've expired on these tiles, weather's our only prophecy. Scrubbed of metaphors, your equable glance tells me zilch about gore absorbed from a floor or face. Ally whose exit never cracked the ticker, no one I know's violence gets stored up to make spring's rising temps, relationship's put out-eyes, lit's scorched Petrarchan martyrs. Pulp bibles and best cellar gods, how will you ward off my fever and braille?

Have You Checked the Children?

Oohs and ahhs from a nonparental unit just stoke the seething newborn's inferno. Chubby dukes hailstoning shoulders and jumping jack tootsies trampling the lap, to him I'm milkless as crack-rock or a moo-juice carton cow jumping over the moon. The fever grinds out jewels that even your bandages weep. Virgin territory do not two genetic lonelinesses make: already he's a pro at steamrolling Rockabyes, his bones before words staking their real-estate claim in gum.

Mirror

A stone's throw kills mirror's two birds. Prettiest pleaser meets Prince who doesn't give a damn about distinctions, just wants to mount the arsenic-white narcoleptic in her glass capsule. Necessity tweaked by later versions in which Envy of course survives, advancing the plot. Demise in the banishment and furnace shoes. Scaffolding, brick, demolition--paid to the facade. Through twinning engine outing psychos that quiver in a lift's blind corner, my shot to run like hell, my proviso for the subject and object closer to disappearance. Mind's eye double vision that goes from huff and puff and blow my glass house down and back to permanent object and good on paper.

Mad

Dr. Funk comes up with vitamins. Saves the children, starves the cold. In the Bedlam do all want a Bonaparte? Lone fringes lick their fingers after eating Napoleons.

Surgical Reflections

Numbers go numb, dumb trumps lonesome, morphine's a damp gown. Scraps for the dingo, gauze bale of beats that screech where the night-owl nurse takes my breath away. AWOL my sterile flynn, MIA my Rasputin who cleaned my revolting body, my revolution body. Who hid the Body when Brain drinks Ether. Tense confusion; remembership drive's a chapter 11. Pulse just sweeps back back in whitecaps like dishwasher water, again in the state of Back, Back—as in count, not come.

Promissory Note

I'll be a good boy, I'll be a nice boy—one hundred yards at all times between you and me, just one sweet from the day-door of the advent calendar. No extras from central nervous system. Five hundred yards and counting. Five hundred years, if that's all it takes. No lonelyhearts note, no explosives. And, Leibchen, you've been awfully good too, a law unto yourself, at attrition a genius. But I here I go again, speaking ill of the undead when I should just shut the fuck up. (Reader, don't try this at home. Viewer depression advised.) To the letter of the law I'll listen, I promise, I'll wash the checks and change my Itunes, in my poems if not in life I'll burn effigies not exes, so many ways to skin the nice kitty yowling on the fire escape but I won't try, I'll keep the babies' breath safe by not inviting babies. Nice kitty, tuxedo stray, no crone's familiar, what's a missing ear, what's a missing squeeze? Goody Jones, Goody Me: how soon the Goody becomes a burnwitch. To the letter of the law listening. I'll hold my horses; they won't trample anyone. We don't call it blood, do we, we call it wisdom, the impacted tooth no fairy wants so swallow it instead.

Canine Songs

All the tricks I learned to not be alone: to bitch or not to bitch, retrieve, Mommy's dogs are a barking, play dead, roll over and rove, nip, bad boy no bite. I understand tone. I understand a helluva lot more than tone. Now that I'm wormed and unreformed, extract my microchip, full-moon howl the house where I grew eunuch and arthritic while the children remained children. Yawning and stretching into its tatty pickpocket robe, Love blubbered for its own albatrosses—they hung pinned, like professional laundry or old school paparrazi candor shots, from a roped, wobbly horizon—and to give itself a smile every day or so it dangled gristle, begged me to beg. Wishes outlasting bones. Caesar a pack-leader.

Wireless

My rollover minutes running out, my nights and weekends not truly unlimited, passcode invalid, underground searches in vain for service or self, please try again then the unit dies, my SIMpleton card gets lost, get the plan upgraded, more minutes, pictures, live aspect ratio autofellatio on audio and video, delete the excess messages of text cuz memory's 100% full, words fall apart, you becomes the letter or the forbidden turn, God forbid now I become an emoticoniclast, let me call u from my land-line while my lifeline still runs long, these voicemails have come faraway for their 21 day save, double fortnight a coach once took delivering epistle, can't we put to death bad-news instant messengers, press star or pound to strike or keep, lock my drunken-dialing keypad, change my ringtone to mimic a species on the endangered list, alter the phone's wallpaper to the stormy-toned forest and the pixilated city where bad numbers and prank calls, ID restricted, still trickle through. Human voices arouse us, flood may blanket my entire contact list, a clone Noah chucking a million handsets from his deck, ravens and doves he'll keep buzzing till someone says pronto.

Goth-Rock Youth

No Memorial Park for defunct gothrock clubs: Voodoo, Eldritch, Necronomicon, all ten years folded. Hitched now and towheaded, the Goth rock fans still wear Dracula black. Only the Goth from Sunset Park wears navy-blue; she's somewhere between the extremes. "I'm older now. I wear gray and blue, like a civil warrior." What's Sunset Park like, I want to know. She says, "It might be called Park Between Dog and Wolf. Have I taken some terrible pictures." Her theory: black protects mourners. The graveyards were sets; the DJs in the nightclubs experimented like mad scientists with us, pouring one sound into another, frenzying us closer. On the dance floor, we drank vinegar to make ourselves look paler by daylight. Acid and mescaline regressed us; we made churches and congregations with our fingers, like kindergartners. do. In record-breaking July, Carmela the Ultra Goth from Metropolitan Avenue leaked white makeup on the pavement near the Astor Cube, which two diminutive Japanese women were putting their shoulder to. A Bizarro world too much to spin. Talking to Carmela, with my Fire Hydrant Red Insane Stain hair dribbled down my neck like zigzags in an Easter Egg. The bouncers certified our fake ID's and stamped us like human visas, and Sunday mornings, too late for church, we woke to fading tattoo faces on the roofs of our hands.

Family Album

The Mansons tended a community clothing pile at Barker and Spahn. Pick the flowergirls, dig up creepycrawlers, leave something witchy. The air of the City of Angels grew ripe with Tate and Labianca during the unlovable summer of fear. Old Blue Eyes went into hiding, Mia missing in action. In the hall of piggy justice, the family were the superfriends and the legion of doom. Sadie giggled. Katie sketched. Leslie looked bored. Supermanson X'd myself from the world because to him it was Kryptonite. Only Predator-to-Mr.-Nice-Guy Squeaky's free four helter skelters later.

The Descending

To go to hell, simply swivel back head like Regan McNeil. Peep at vaporized Sodom or the zombie girl on the path, else play strip-poker on Sabbath, or munch certain Winesap or pomegranate. One false move for a token, morally bankrupt treasury of false notes and moves. Must be some precipitation in hell from all that goddamn crying, bring a Totes. But no, only purgatory, an all night launderette, all you can breathe hot air from the spin-dryers never empty, bleached linen restrictions. Here we all get stoned on the worthless drugs of Everlast and Neverend, no conceptions, no immaculates. All this finger to the bone work just for some off-color clothes? Next life I'll be chopped liver, keep my devil's playground pristine, a birthday suit my Sunday best.

III. Rooms

1. A Brighter, Superior Box

Handle with Care. Care of. Car-Rt Sort. Return to sender. He learned those terms when he was a kid, getting the mail from his parent's box. The mailbox was knocked down repeatedly by boys in cars who rode around with baseball bats. Each time, his parents replaced it with something brighter and superior. No matter how dignified or indomitable the box, boys knocked it down, and mail still came for the previous tenant. His parents never moved. They stayed in that cottage throwing that woman's mail out, buying new mailboxes, refusing to let these setbacks change their plans.

2. Grand Prize Winner

For the twentieth or thirtieth time, he's turned in the paperwork with the postal service. The latest request hasn't been honored yet, and no mail has reached him here. If he'd won a fortune and the authorities in charge of fortunes tried to contact him with a congratulatory telegram, he would have no way of knowing it.

3. 1-800-HANDOUT

The mail should come to a studio apartment in Long Island City. His friend who rents the apartment is in Bangkok for the entire month with her boyfriend. She wanted to move to New Mexico but settled for Long Island City, which is a version of the desert. Phone-order mattress warehouses, billboards for expensive vehicles, an elevated freeway he can hear and see every waking moment. All his hand-me-down furniture is here, donated from his old places. He thinks that *hand-me-down* makes it sound somewhat invaded, but sexy. Less sterile than *given*.

4. The Earplugs Make the Man

Two cats, one vicious, one rambunctious, both functionally infertile, use the furniture as Territory: they hide under it, claw the fabrics, mark table-legs with chin-rubs, claim surprisingly hard desktops for periods of sleep that seem more like narcolepsy than napping. Territory is not property. He knows the difference by now. He thinks giving up everything means he can have even more places in his future, he can keep changing the view, reading the books on other people's shelves. That's territory. People have described him as *territorial*. He likes to invade, but shrinks back from being invaded. Also he's been called cold. He should come from that place in Canada, not a province, not a place-name, not an oxymoron place-name, like Long Island City. Northwest Territory: arctic tundra, uninhabitable. He only feels warm for the wrong reasons. He thinks they're the right reasons: two arms around him, why should he pretend to feel something when he's paid for his own past insincerity? Supermarket aisles pour out their aspartame love songs. He wears ear plugs sometimes to ward off these infectious tunes, even when he is in love.

5. After Watching Certain Documentaries on the Manson Family

Like a crime-scene technician, he requires too much proof. Such a call for evidence rules out people saying things like the following: Look at Him, He Loves Love, Doesn't He Just Love to Be in Love?

6. Customs and Immigration

His body is a kind of property. For example, his mother told him when he was little how other people might try to touch his private parts. When they were children and fought all the time, his cousin told him to get lost. *Get off my property.* The cousin's hand was at his crotch whenever he said it.

7. The Gift of Clean Sheets

Though he has little right, he wants to say and do the same thing when his predecessor, the former housesitter, his other friend, drops by with the sheets she's washed. Why wash the sheets? It's considerate, but why bother? Is she covering something up? Did she bring someone here? She would have told him. He thinks she should have used her opportunity to bring someone here: she lives with her parents, something he could never handle. In his own way he's just as homeless, but not as familial.

8. Virgins

He goes to make the bed, picks up the clean sheets, but the friend says, No, Wait. She insists that there is a specific way to make it and she must help him. The skirt must adorn the bottom frame, the fitted sheet must be folded around the mattress just so. She was a virgin until she was twenty-five. She doesn't know how he envies that fact. He wishes he could go back again to not knowing how to kiss, how to produce the overhyped conclusions. The borders become so obvious again, whenever it's over and it's time for numbers and pleasantries, when all the secrets of the other have to be sussed out. He holds back from orgasm so often with this other or that other, to keep the sweet, sweet arrangement going as long as possible.

9. No Laser Surgery Necessary

Used to carrying unwieldy things from his all his apartment-hopping, he lifts the bulky mattress off the bed. It's stained with ink, not blood or semen or piss. Pens used to explode in his pockets in grade school: a bid for attention by means of self-humiliation. *If you won't mark me, I'll mark myself.* Now they explode on the bed when he leaves them there uncapped when writing something he hopes will be published or at least read by someone else. Posturepedic tattoos. His body has no such insignia: is it property or territory? Does he really know the difference?

10. The Mission

The friend gets to work on the skirt. It has a tear from her washer. She ripped it the way the infertile cats rip something they love, the way his writing hand suffers more cuts than any part of his body. Washing and dropping off the sheets was just a pretext. She loves this place, wants it for herself though she refused to stay the whole night when she was sitting. She hates him for being here, hates her family for barricading her future. There, finally the fitted sheet is on, the skirt is wrapped so the rip faces the wall, it's his bed made Her Way but he doesn't care.

11. Georgia O'Keeffe Stayed Up All Night to Sew a Lining in Alfred Stieglitz's Coffin

Their argument over making the bed outlasts the actual making.

12. Bonnie & Clyde, If They Went Nowhere

They sit at the table and smoke cigarettes from the Bible Belt, where they're cheaper. He perceives in her advice that she thinks him incapable of the simplest things. He is an aphasiac who has to be told how to turn a key, how to lock a window. She's "trying to be helpful." She helps so much she won't leave though it's late at night. The desert-neighborhood has a way of blurring the sensible hours from the fugitive ones.

13. Yawn

Why doesn't he say, Leave, already? Why does he apologize for how late is? Why is this such a requirement? On the other hand, why is staying up when everyone else is asleep so shameful? She doesn't leave immediately.

14. In this Year of History, Watergate

They find some memories that make them laugh. Remember the guy who rock-climbed down the building? They talk about the other friend, the one in Thailand. All three were born the year of Nixon's resignation. Funny, they say, no one born our year has gotten married, who we know of. Even that makes them laugh, sort of.

15. A View from the Curb

Finally she does get up from the table. He walks her down to her car. He loves her despite her advice, or because of it. He loves that, before she pulls from the curb, she must see he is entirely capable of inserting the key in the door. This is no cheap metaphor: they've never slept together, sexually or otherwise. This is about proving himself separate, alert, indefatigably self-sufficient. He hates those words, their pretensions, as soon as he fits them to his description. And proving them gets him nowhere but back inside, where the expressway lives up to its reputation: major artery. Perhaps desert is too strong a word to describe where he is.

16. Prayer to St. Someone

A few hours of television, dated sitcoms and ads for those who have lost all mobility. Such a condition terrifies him: having to ride on a motorized cart, please let it never happen to him. This he prays to whatever being his agnosticism will accommodate. He thinks about people in fugue states who drift away from their families, from every weight and anchor they've known. They start lives. New lives? Maybe they're not really so new after all. Somewhere inside one of the brain's lobes the details endure. Patterns repeat. It's not all hopeless or stultifying, as long as there's something to be added. He thinks about files he's deleted on computers. He lost his senior thesis due to a virus, but a computer programmer recovered it. Deletion stopped being such a persuasive or frightening thing after that.

17. Wet Dream

He's never had one. He lies down on his stomach so that his head, limbs and penis touch the sheet, which smells of nothing at all, and the tattooed mattress, the contents of the mattress which he heard described on a television program once as a fascinating, awful combination of dead skin and microbial organisms. Still it's all owned and contained and occupied. He closes his eyes and moves forward into the mattress until the sheet is wet, and he has to turn over.

18. Pledge of Allegiance

He'd rather think about random things than the future, or get going with the dreams he has when he sleeps. Lately they've been annoying typical, all about missing the exam at school. The teachers he liked never show up. The teachers who do show up haven't changed much, personality-wise. Superior, condescending, and intent only on keeping the herd in check, they notice him only when he falls out of line.

19. Sometimes the Phone

Is it an automated telemarketer, is it a person dialing a wrong number? Is it the woman from the sex directory who told him she would phone-fuck him until he lost his voice?

20. Premonitions of Power

They look at him as if he were a slide of glass, as if he were just a speck, a specimen. Onion skin that has to be stained, an amoeba skidding along in its ignorant, unlikely dimension. They looked at him the same way, back in school. Maybe that's why they were so smug, when they were real people and not just the brain's stock footage: they knew he would dream about them, because everyone dreams about school.

21. Subconscious Revenge on the Teachers

Some of them have grown extra fingers, wear smashed eyeglasses, or say things that make no sense.

22. Mansion

He will never have 22 rooms all at once.

23. Because the Monks Were the First to See the Microscopic World

The teachers visit him no matter where he escapes; they'll kill or cure, slit open the mattress and drag him over to the microscope to see where his old skin ends up. Those little oblong shapes he sees are called cells.

Ideas Beyond Conventional

www.ingramcontent.com/pod-product-compliance
Lightning Source LLC
Chambersburg PA
CBHW060503080526
44584CB00015B/1526